SPIKING V
AND OTHER EXCITING B
GW01605601
GREG FREEMAN
TEXT
IAN HEATH
CARTOONS
CORGI
OOOOH!
AAAH!!

SPIKING VIKINGS

A CORGI BOOK 0 552 99253 4

First publication in Great Britain

PRINTING HISTORY

Corgi edition published 1986

Corgi Books are published by Transworld Publishers Ltd., 61-63 Uxbridge Road, Ealing, London W5 5SA, in Australia by Transworld Publishers (Aust.) Pty. Ltd., 15-23 Helles Avenue, Moorebank, NSW 2170,and in New Zealand by Transworld Publishers (N.Z.) Ltd., Cnr. Moselle and Waipareira Avenues, Henderson, Auckland.

Made and printed in West Germany by Mohndruck, Gütersloh

NOUGHTS & CROSSES

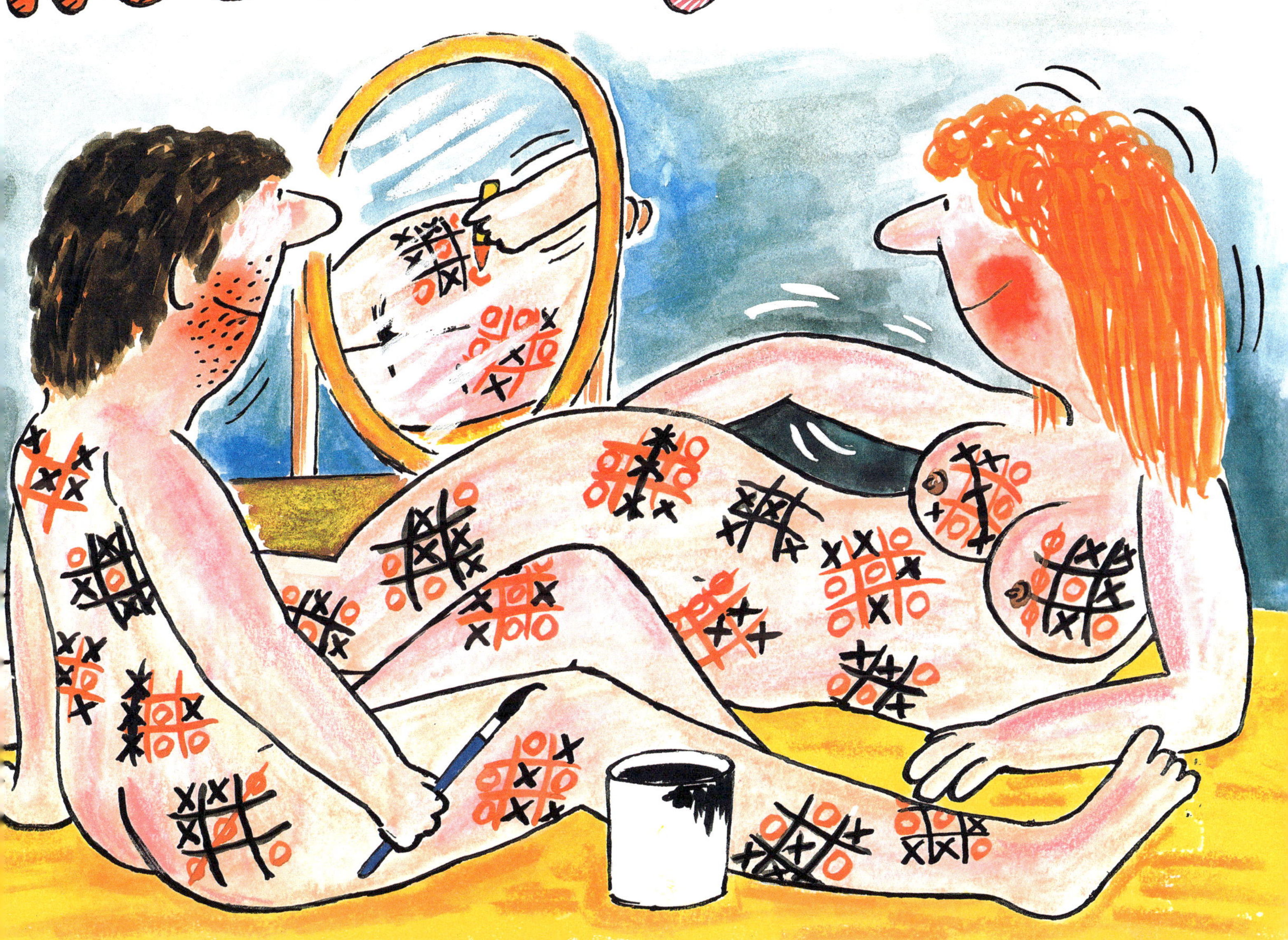

LEAP-FROG

PLAYERS

6 or more.

PREPARATION

One player is chosen as the 'frog'. He is blindfolded and made to bend over. From the remaining players, a 'princess' is chosen.

PLAY

The 'princess' now leaps over the 'frog' and the 'frog' has to try and guess the identity of the 'princess'. If he is correct, he is allowed to go outside and kiss her. If he tries to do more than that, he isn't a frog but a toad.

SPLAT!!
AAARGH!!
SNAP!
CRUNCH!

CLOUD HOPPING

EQUIPMENT

9 pieces of furniture (inc. the bed) which represent nine clouds.

PREPARATION

Players split into pairs and hold hands. The 'clouds' are arranged, like stepping stones, around the room.

ORDER OF PLAY

Starting from 'cloud 1' (the bed), the couples must move from 'cloud' to 'cloud', without touching the floor or breaking hands.

END OF PLAY

The couple who get to 'cloud 9' first win. Of course there will be players who'll reach 'cloud 9' without ever leaving the bed. They're disqualified.

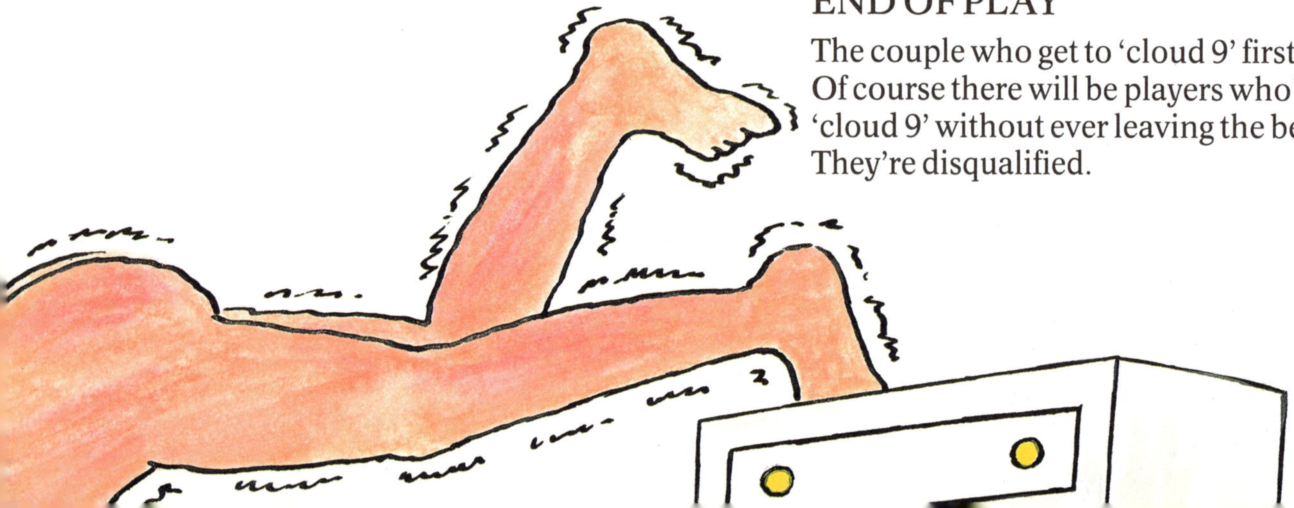

EEEOO!!

MINI-HA!-HA!

PLAYERS

Two: Squaw Minnehaha. Brave Minnetonka.

OBJECT OF THE GAME

Self control.

PLAY

Squaw Minnehaha tests Brave Minnetonka by taking off all her clothes. Brave Minnetonka must show great restraint or take a cold shower.

Brave Minnetonka now tests Squaw Minnehaha by coming out of the cold shower. Squaw Minnehaha must show great restraint and not laugh at brave's mini-tonka.

PASSION KILLER

PLAYERS

Three: 2 in bed. 1 in a telephone box.

AFRICAN ADVENTURE

PREPARATION

One player decides that they want to take up the position of Missionary to the Okanookoo tribe.

PLAY

Having taken up their missionary position, the other player now has to try and persuade them to take up a more adventurous position.

PASS THE ORANGE

EQUIPMENT

One orange.

PREPARATION

Players sit in a circle around the bed. Then one player tucks the orange under their chin.

PLAY

The object is for players to pass the orange around the circle using only their chins. Any player who drops the orange is out of the game.

Warning: It is unwise to play this game in the dark as someone always eats the orange.

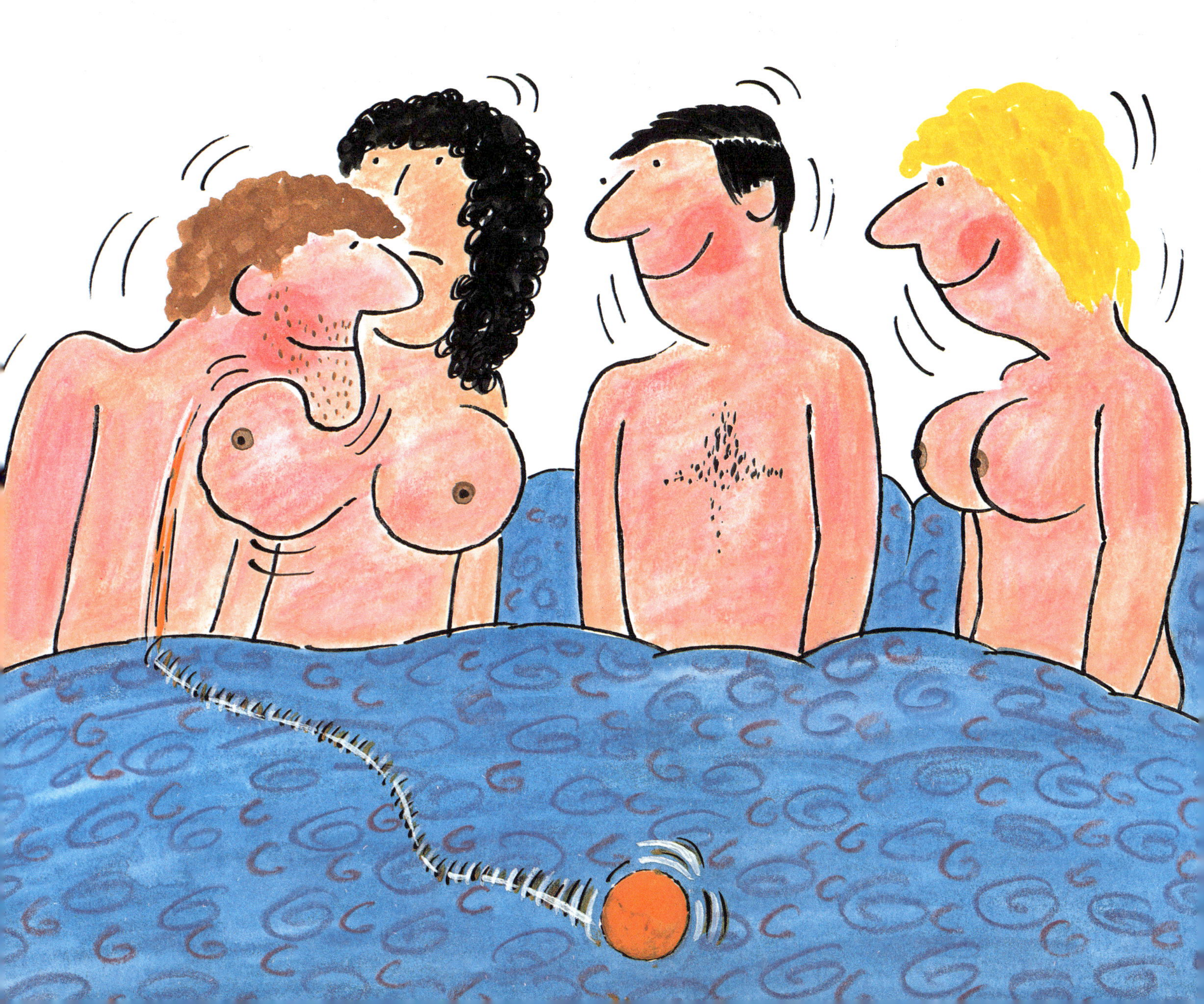

TICKLE MY FANCY

PLAYERS
Two.

EQUIPMENT
2 feather dusters
2 books

PREPARATION
Each player balances a book on their head.

PLAY
The object is to see who can balance the book the longest, whilst at the same time trying to unsettle their opponent by tickling their fancy.

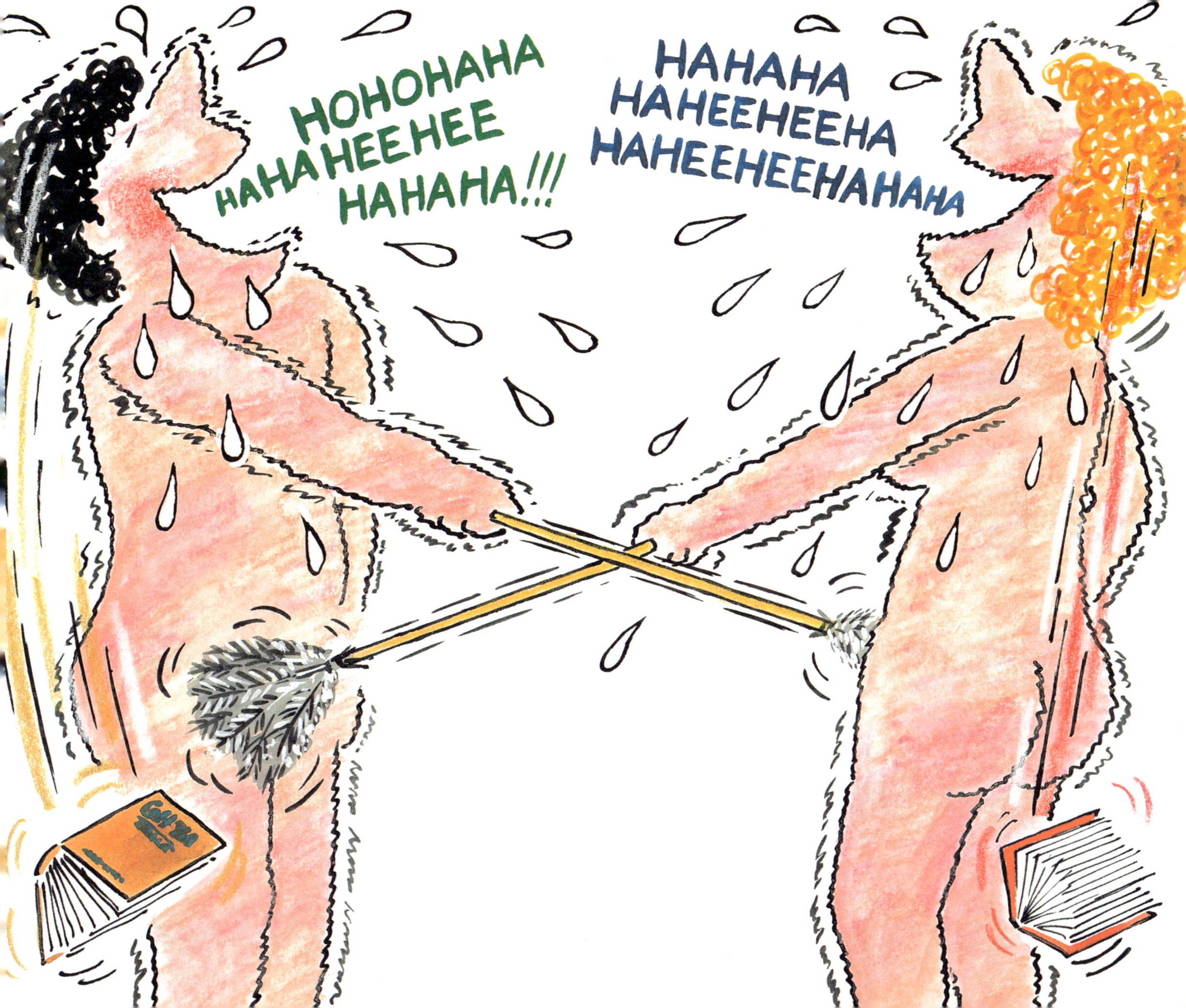
HOHOHAHA
HAHAHEEHEE
HAHAHA!!!
HAHAHA
HAHEEHEEHA
HAHEEHEEHAHAHA

PLAYERS

Four.

EQUIPMENT

3 wooden spoons

ORDER OF PLAY

The spoons are placed on the bed. The players all step back three paces. The starter drops his handkerchief and the four players try to grab one of the three spoons.
The player who fails to get a spoon is now known as a 'Billy Sugger' and has to perform a forfeit.

WILLIAM TELL

PLAYERS
Two.

EQUIPMENT
A bow, a quiver of rubber suckered arrows, a very big apple.

ORDER OF PLAY
One player balances the apple upon their head. The other player now shoots arrows at the apple.

END OF PLAY
When the apple gets hit or when the other player gets fed up with being peppered by little rubber suckers.

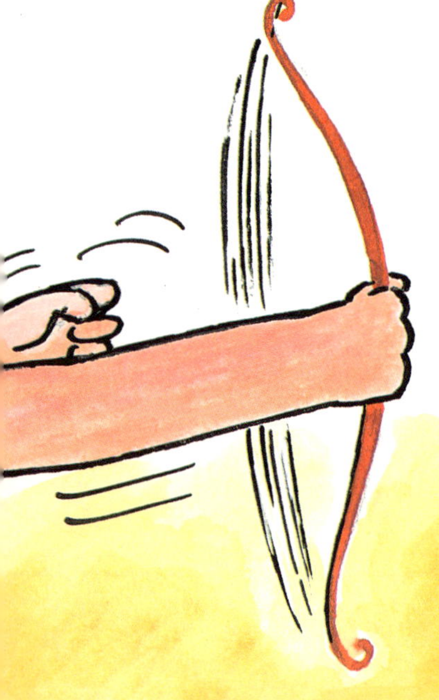

PLAYERS

Two or more.

EQUIPMENT

Large quantity of balloons, Viking helmets.

PREPARATION

Balloons are pinned to the ceiling. Players strap on their helmets and climb up onto the bed.

PLAY

On the command "Valhalla!" players must bounce up and down on the bed and try to spike as many balloons as possible.

END OF PLAY

When all the balloons have been burst, when the bed collapses or when the neighbour downstairs calls the Police.

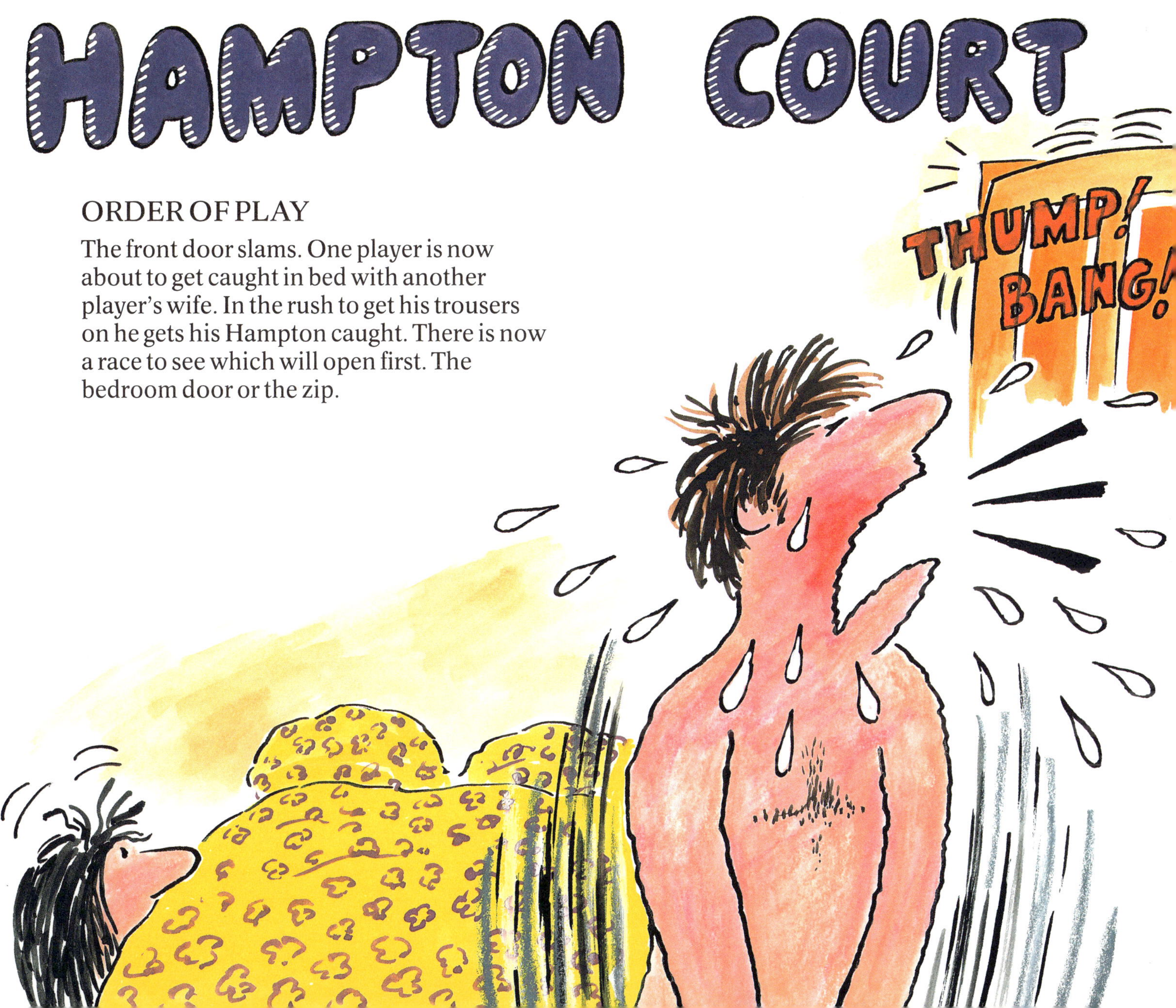

ORDER OF PLAY

The front door slams. One player is now about to get caught in bed with another player's wife. In the rush to get his trousers on he gets his Hampton caught. There is now a race to see which will open first. The bedroom door or the zip.

PREPARATION

One player is appointed leader and the other players arrange themselves around the bed.

PLAY

The leader now orders the other players to make various actions – eg. touching their toes. If the leader starts the order with the words "O'Grady says", then the players must obey the order. If the leader omits to say "O'Grady says", then the players must disobey and touch any other player where the hell they like.

LENGTH OF PLAY

Game ends when the leader reaches £200 in bribes.

OH DEAR! – I'M SURE
I SAID "O'GRADY SAYS"!

AGAIN!!
MMM!!
OOO!!
AAAH!
MORE!
EEE!
OOH!

SNAKES AND LADDERS

PLAYERS

Two.

EQUIPMENT

Twin beds, a ladder.

PREPARATION

The ladder is arranged so that it spans from bed to bed.

OBJECT

Each player is a snake. Travelling in opposite directions, they have to go across the ladder, across each other and reach their opponent's bed first.

Warning: Do not be surprised if some players take advantage of their opponents in the middle of the ladder...what can you expect from a snake?

AAARGH!!

THAT'S NO GHERKIN!

PLAYERS

Four: 1 Customs Official
3 Passengers (one of whom is a smuggler)

PREPARATION

The 'smuggler' hides a gherkin upon their person.

PLAY

The passengers now present themselves to the 'customs official' who will frisk each of them. The 'customs official' must now decide which of them is the 'Gherkin Smuggler'

FLESHPOTS OF MARRAKESH

EQUIPMENT

Silky lingerie

ORDER OF PLAY

One player puts on the equipment and pretends to be a mysterious Courtesan from the East...whilst the other player pretends not to notice.

HAVE YOU PUT THE CAT OUT?

ONE NIGHT STAND

EQUIPMENT
A brown paper bag.

WHOSE BABY?

PLAYERS

Minimum three.

STATUES

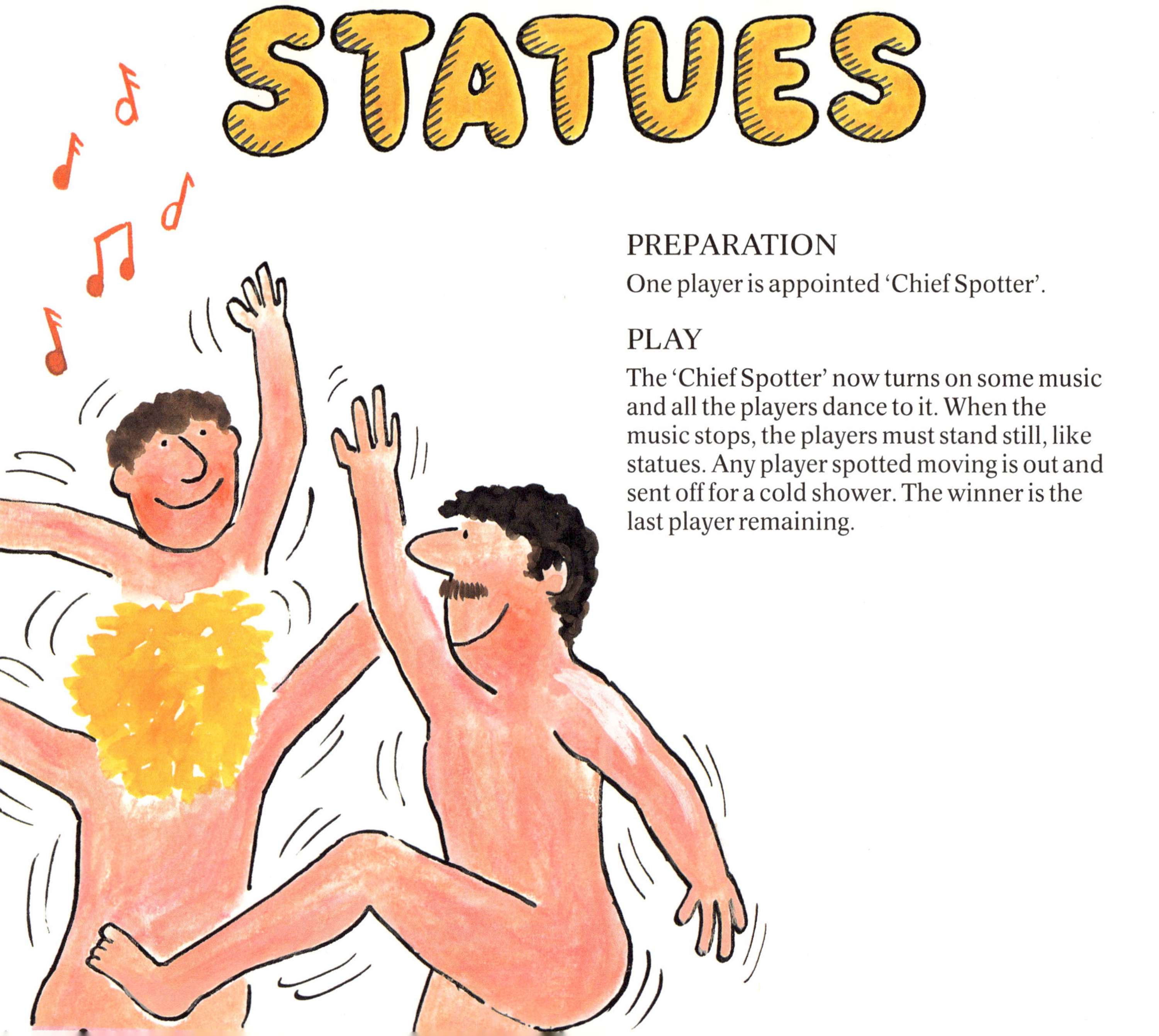

PREPARATION

One player is appointed ‘Chief Spotter’.

PLAY

The ‘Chief Spotter’ now turns on some music and all the players dance to it. When the music stops, the players must stand still, like statues. Any player spotted moving is out and sent off for a cold shower. The winner is the last player remaining.

IT
MOVED!

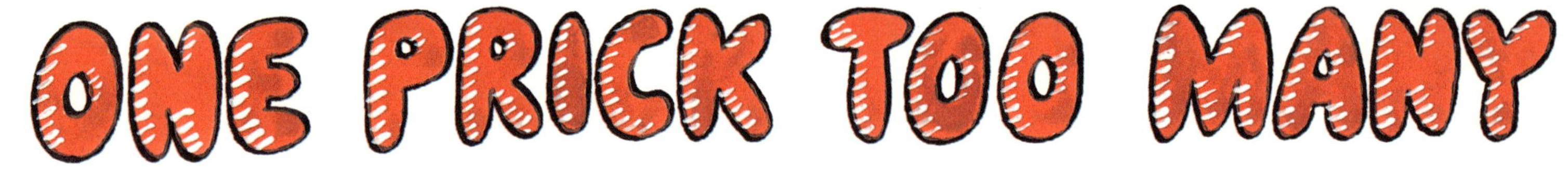

PREPARATION

During the early evening, one player unwraps a new shirt and carelessly scatters the pins over the bed. He then departs for a night on the town.

PLAY

During the early morning, the player returns with another player he has met at a wine bar. They both stagger into bed and, without even trying, start to find the pins.

END OF GAME

When one player runs out of apologies and elastoplast – and the other player runs out of the door.

EQUIPMENT

Large quantity of ring doughnuts.

ORDER OF PLAY

One player holds up a finger. The other player now tries to toss the doughnuts over the upheld finger. Should the tosser find this too difficult, the other player should stick up two fingers.

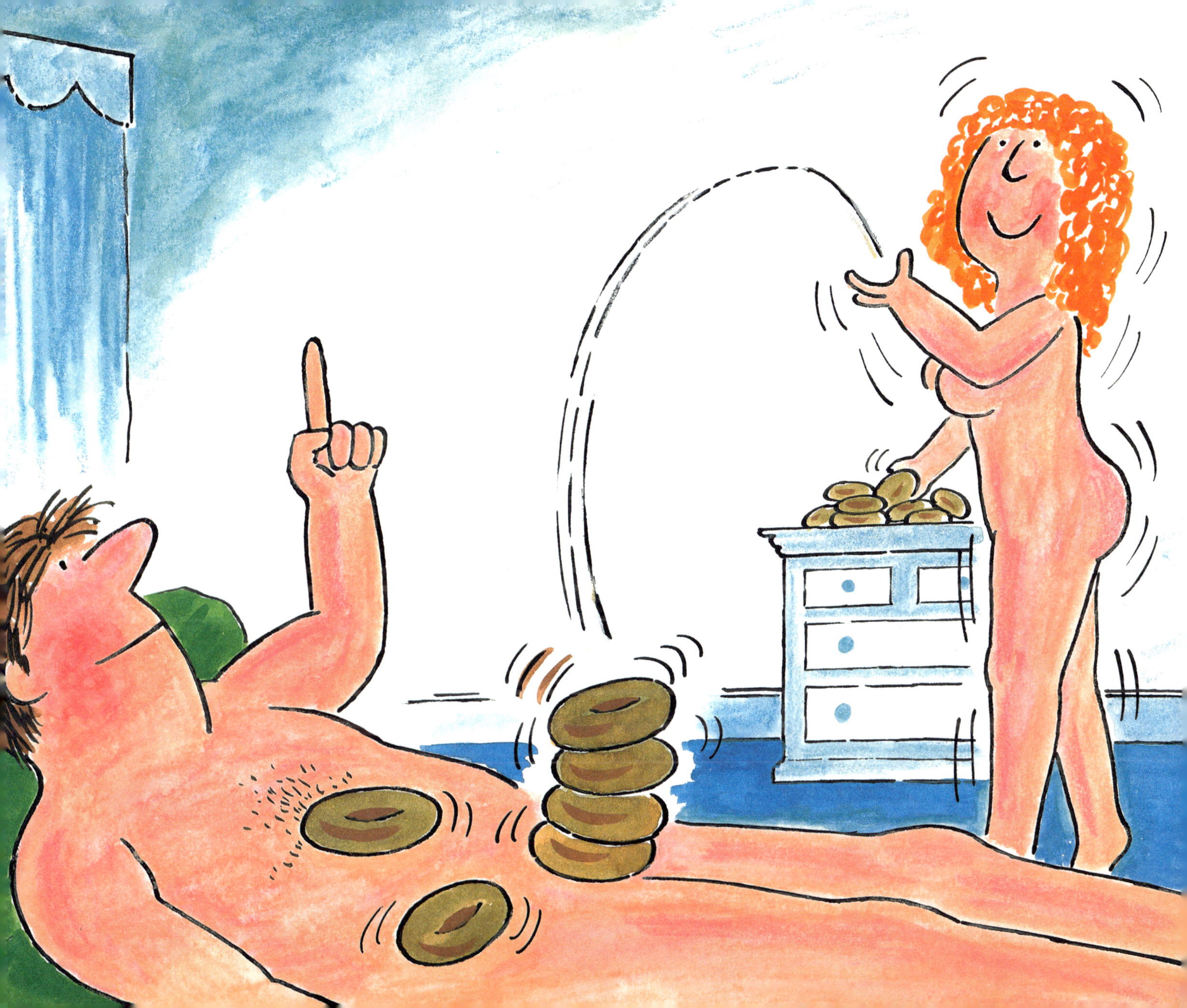

NUTS AND MELONS

PLAYERS

Five or more: 2 or more Nuns, 2 or more Monks, 1 Mother Superior.

EQUIPMENT

A torch, four melons, four bags of nuts, twin beds.

PREPARATION

One bed is the 'Monastery Garden' the other bed is the 'Nunnery Garden'. Players sit in their respective 'gardens' with their garden produce. Mother Superior stands between the 'gardens' and holds the torch. The lights are now turned off.

OBJECT

The 'monks' have to creep over to the 'Nunnery Garden', past Mother Superior and pinch the 'nuns' melons. Mother Superior must try and spot them with the torch. Then it is the 'nuns' turn to sneak over and try and grab the 'monks' nuts.

I LOVE IT!
TOUCH ME!
AGAIN! AGAIN!
WHAT A HANDFUL!!
COR!
ooo000000000!!
AAA!
MY NUTS!
MORE!
LOVELY!
YUMMY!!
LET GO!
MMMMMM!
MORE?
DO IT AGAIN!
EEEEEEE!
WHAT MELONS!
GOT YOU!

AS YOU LIKE IT

THIS IS FOR YOU TO FILL IN

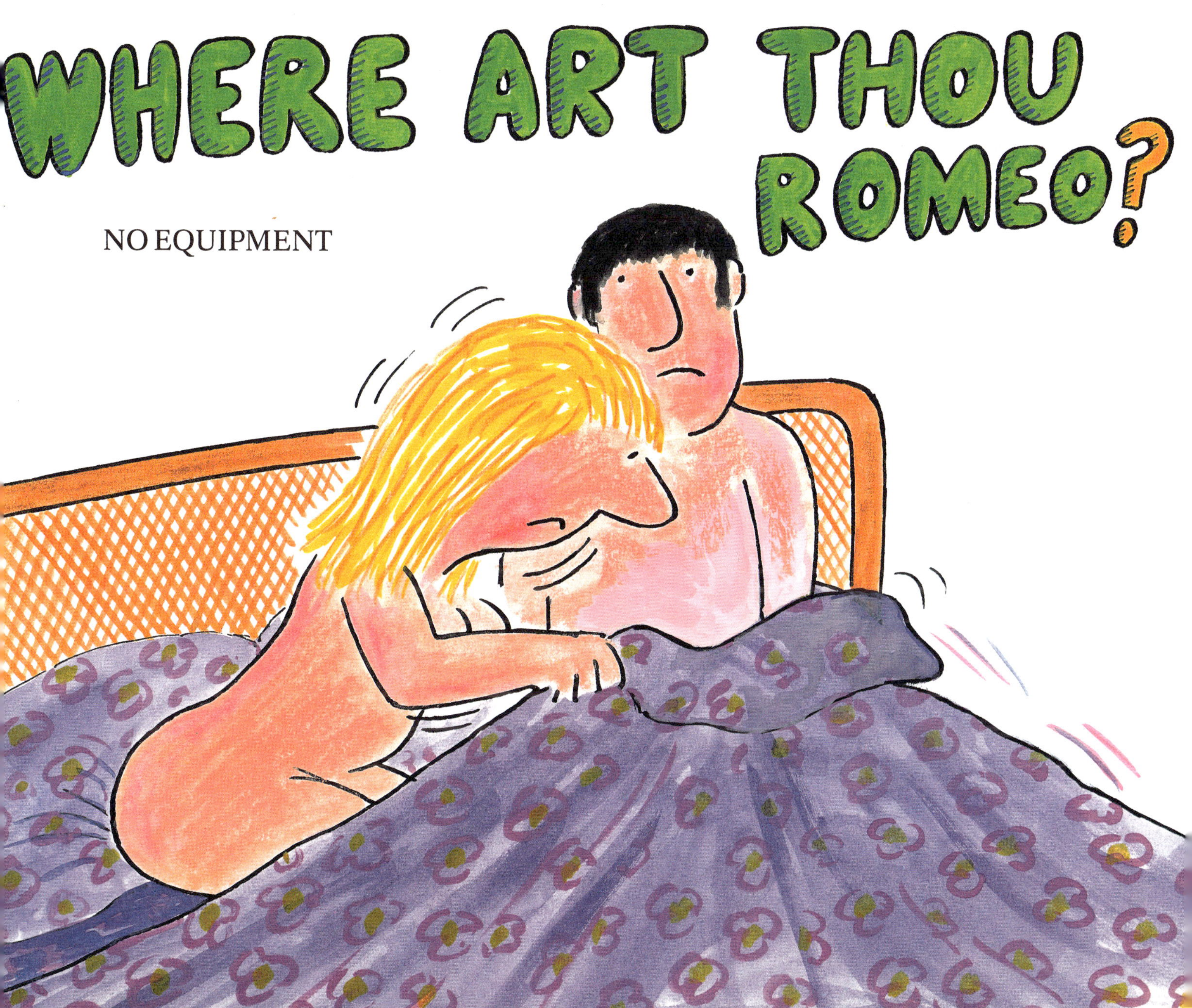
WHERE ART THOU ROMEO?
NO EQUIPMENT

FOAM FUN

EQUIPMENT

Shaving foam, small sticking plasters.

PREPARATION

Unseen by the other players, each player sticks a plaster upon their person. They then conceal the plaster by covering themselves in shaving foam.

PLAY

The object of the game is for players to discover the whereabouts of their opponents plaster by blowing away the foam. Bicycle pumps are not permitted.

WINNER

The player who manages to keep their plaster from being revealed the longest.

LOSER

The player who manages to keep their plaster from being revealed the longest, but precious little else.

BUSHWHACKERS

PLAYERS
Two.

EQUIPMENT
Nine balloons, holly.

PREPARATION
The balloons are scattered around the room. Players arm themselves with a branch of holly.

PLAY
The object of the game is to see who can burst five balloons first, by whacking them with the holly.

Warning: Short sighted players are advised to wear their glasses. What they assume are a couple of pink balloons could well turn out to be their opponent's buttocks.

SQUEALS ON WHEELS

EQUIPMENT

Skateboard
Quantity of wet sponges
Plastic sheet.

PREPARATION

The plastic sheet is laid out over the carpet and the skateboard is placed on top of it. Two players now balance on the skateboard.

PLAY

The object is for the other players to knock the couple off the skateboard by throwing wet sponges at them. The players on the skateboard must not only try and dodge the sponges but also resist the temptation to knock each other off.

EEEEEEK!
WOWEEEEEEE!!

PLAYERS

Two.

EQUIPMENT

2 whistles, string.

PREPARATION

Each player ties a whistle to their ankle. They kneel on the bed facing each other.

PLAY

The object now is for the players to grapple with each other and try to blow their opponent's whistle.

PEEEEEEEP!!

NOT TONIGHT, JOSÉPHINE

EQUIPMENT

One bottle of Napoleon brandy

OOO!! AAA!!

PLAYERS

Two.

There are no particular rules. No particular winner. But the player who cries 'Ooo!' or 'Aaa!' the loudest probably will have enjoyed it the most.

NYMPHS AND SHEPHERDS

PLAYERS

Seven: One wolf, three shepherds, three nymphs.

PREPARATION

The nymphs, O'Connor, O'Malley and O'Maniac, lie on the bed guarded by the three shepherds.

PLAY

The object of the game is for the shepherds to try and stop the wolf jumping on the nymphs, whilst at the same time the nymphs, O'Connor and O'Malley, have to stop the nymph, O'Maniac, jumping on the shepherds.

BANANA FLIPPERS

PLAYERS

Two:
Sea Lion
Zoo Keeper

EQUIPMENT

Pair of flippers, quantity of bananas.

PREPARATION

The 'Sea Lion' puts the flippers on his hands.

PLAY

It is feeding time at the zoo. The 'Zoo Keeper', being slightly bananas, throws bananas at the 'Sea Lion', who will try to catch them with the flippers.

END OF PLAY

Game ends when the 'Sea Lion' catches three bananas or one below the belt.

SMACK!!

I'VE GOT A HEADACHE

PLAYERS

Two: A cave man. A cavewoman.

EQUIPMENT

A bunk bed, a club.

ORDER OF PLAY

The 'caveman' lies on the bottom bunk. The 'cavewoman' lies on the top bunk with the club. 'Caveman' now asks 'cavewoman' if he can join her on the top bunk. To which she relies: "No, I've got a headache"
Being uncouth and unconvinced, he now tries to climb up uninvited. Unperturbed, "cavewoman" fends him off by clonking him on the head with the club.

LENGTH OF PLAY

Game ends when he too, concedes to having a headache.

CLONK!

PLAYERS

Two: Sporty type. Non-sporty type.

EQUIPMENT

A hoola-hoop, 4 pancakes.

PREPARATION

The non-sporty player holds the hoop in one hand and the four pancakes in the other.

PLAY

The object of the race is for the sporty player to leap through the hoop, crawl under the bed, out the other side, touch all four walls and jump back on the bed before the non-sporty player can eat the four pancakes.

CRUNCH!

PING THE DING-A-LING

PLAYERS

Two.

EQUIPMENT

A bell, a pea-shooter, quantity of dried peas.

ORDER OF PLAY

One player holds out the bell. The other player now tries to ring the bell by blowing peas at it. Once the bell has been rung, players change places.

DRIED PEAS

OOOW!!

PLAYERS

Two or more:
1 Jailer
1 or more convicts.

EQUIPMENT

Balloons on strings

PREPARATION

The 'convicts' tie a ball and chain (balloon on a string) to their ankles.

PLAY

The 'convicts' have escaped from jail and run wildly around the bedroom. The 'jailer' now has to recapture the 'convicts' by stamping on their 'balls' and bursting them.

THE
END